SLUG PREVENTION
The Natural Way
by Chris Morris

This book is copyright protected, and it is only for personal use. You cannot amend, distribute, sell, use, quote or paraphrase any part of the content within the book without the written consent of the author or copyright owner.

Every effort has been made to make this book as complete and accurate as possible. Although the author and publisher have prepared this publication with the greatest of care, and every effort has been made to ensure its accuracy, we assume no responsibility or liability for errors, inaccuracies or omissions. You assume all risks associated with using the advice given below, with a full understanding that you, solely, are responsible for anything that may occur as a result of putting this information into action in any way, and regardless of your interpretation of the advice.

The purpose of this book is to educate. The author and publisher do not warrant that the information contained in the book is fully complete and shall not be responsible for any errors or omissions. The author and publisher shall have neither liability nor responsibility to any person or entity with respect to any loss or damage caused or alleged to be caused directly or indirectly by this book, nor do we make any claims or promises of your ability to achieve the same, or any positive, results as asserted by using any of this information.

© Copyright 2017 Chris Morris. All Rights Reserved

SLUG PREVENTION
The Natural Way
Your comprehensive Slugpedia for getting rid of slugs - naturally

Welcome to your guide to over 100 methods of slug control without using the chemical treatments which may be bad for wildlife and the environment. Some chemical poisons may kill slugs very effectively, but they will also have a pretty detrimental effect on their predators.

Extensive research has gone into this compilation, which has drawn together information from many sources to provide an A-Z index, which has been cross-referenced for ease of use. There is no single silver bullet which is guaranteed to get rid of slugs every time, in every garden, in every part of the world. You will probably find that different combinations will work best for you, depending upon your particular circumstances.

Do please bear in mind that no matter how much you may dislike slugs in your garden, no-one should wish for absolute slug extinction. Slug control is the desired aim. After all, slugs are a valuable food source for many creatures, including the hedgehog, amphibians, and many birds.

Eradicating all slugs from your garden would also be detrimental to the soil's health. Slugs are in fact very efficient at recycling organic material and helping to enrich soil in a similar fashion to compost. It is important to strike a balance. There is some merit in having a few slugs around to act as mini-composters for your garden, as well as being food for beneficial creatures.

It is vital to maintain the right balance of your garden friends, the bees, butterflies, ladybugs, neuroptera such as lacewings and all the rest, so be careful that slug control doesn't create a detrimental knock-on effect.

Don't rely on just one of the following methods. Some work in certain areas better than others, some work with particular types of slug and not others, and combining methods as part of a varied approach is by far the best, according to your own circumstances. Persevere, be consistent, test and test again. The answer is here. The question is, which is the one for you?

N.B.
For ease of use I refer mainly to slugs throughout this book, although the vast majority of methods will equally apply to snails.

The A-Z Slugpedia

This book has been designed for fast cross-referencing. All entries are alphabetized, and related subjects are in italics and underlined, to indicate that you can flick through to a relevant section on another page.

Aluminum Foil (*aluminium foil*)
You can try this as an experiment around one or two of your prized plants. The reason you may wish to experiment at first is that there are other deterrents later in this book which use different methods, and this may perhaps be the least attractive and organic of them all. However, if you find that your slimy garden guests are significantly deterred by this method then you can ramp it up.

So, the simple idea of using aluminum foil as a deterrent starts with a preparation of your preferred garden mulch method. Then mix into it several strips of aluminum foil. This is a material that slugs do not respond to very well, and as long as there is sufficient concentration of these strips to keep them at bay your plants should remain unmolested by the mollusk.

Aluminum Sulfate (*aluminium sulphate*)
This is an extra deterrent for your arsenal, but it tends only to be effective against small slugs.

There have been various scare stories in the press about excessive exposure to this chemical compound, but it continues to be used in water purification.

Although connections between aluminum and dementia have been investigated in the past the results were inconclusive and few scientists today believe that it poses any threat in regular use. You are unlikely to overuse it in your garden, but nevertheless it is certainly worth bearing in mind, and we do not recommend its use over other, more natural methods.

Slugs certainly don't like it, and if you are concerned then be sure to use in moderation (when slugs are particularly active, after rain for example), and avoid contact with seedlings.

Ash
Slugs and snails dislike dry, abrasive, surfaces so you can build up an inch-high, three-inch wide barrier of ashes distributed around your entire garden, or just your tastiest plants, to deter the pests. Obviously this protective barrier may be unrealistic for very large gardens, and it will need to be replaced quite frequently following rain, but it is quite easy to do if you have regular access to ash or cinders.

However, you will find that excessive use tends to increase the alkaline level of the soil. As is so often the case, it is a question of balance, and you may redress this by also using several of the other methods listed here, such as _aluminum sulfate_, _hair_, and a grassy mulch sprinkled with _pine needles._

Badgers

These animals will prefer to eat your garden-friendly earthworms rather than slugs, but they are not going to turn down a slug smorgasbord if your garden is alive with slugs. In general a badger is likely to harm your lawn and also eat any slug-eating hedgehogs in the vicinity, so they are not really to be encouraged. Nevertheless, if you want to be rid of slugs then a badger can certainly help you out.

Bark Chippings

This form of barrier is unlikely to work in isolation, because although slugs and snails dislike the movement of the chippings as they slither over them there is little to stop them from taking the easier route by finding their way through beneath the bark.

However, if you add smaller, shredded bark chippings, particularly pine bark, as a secondary barrier above a scratchy mulch or other deterrent surface referred to throughout this book then you will have double the resistance. You must out-think the slug!

You may also use regular bark chippings as a means of trapping slugs, since they will tend to hide beneath the bark. Concentrate the area for this trap in an accessible corner of your garden, spread the bark chippings not less than 6 inches square, then investigate the slug population ready for handpicking the next morning.

Barriers

There are plenty of commercial barriers available, (you can read reviews of some of the best ones on our website *www.slugprevention.com*) but there are also a multitude of home-prepared obstacles which you can place in a slug's path. Scratchy stuff will help, as will copper, plastic bottles around stems - and a fly screen!

Each of these methods is described in more detail separately throughout this book (see below, on the following page). What you should always bear in mind, however, is that for every slug above ground there are likely to be a further five underground, and if the determined slug can't go over it then it will go under it, so while most barriers act as a deterrent the best ones are those which can spread right up against the plant stem without damaging it.

The good news is that many of the underground slugs prefer to stay right where they are, grinding up dead material and cultivating your soil for you, and are not be burrowing underground purely to circumvent your barrier!

Here are some examples of barriers and deterrents which you can read about in more depth throughout this book:

Aluminum Foil - _Aluminum Sulfate_ - _Artemisia Leaves_ - _Ash_ - _Bark Chippings_ - _Bordeaux Mixture_ - _Cat Litter_ - _Cinders_ - _Coffee_ - _Companion Planting_ - _Copper_ - _Cotton Wool_ - _Diatomaceous Earth_ - _Dry Surfaces_ - _Epsom Salts_ - _Fly Screen_ - _Flour_ - _Garlic_ - _Geranium Leaves_ - _Ginger_ - _Grease_ - _Hair_ - _Herbs_ (aromatic) - _Horseradish_ - _Lava Rock_ - _Lavender_ - _Light_ - _Lime_ - _Lint_ - _Mulch Deterrents_ - _Mullein Leaves_ - _Mugwort_ - _Neem Oil_ - _Oak Leaves_ - _Petroleum Jelly_ - _Pine Needles_ - _Pistachio Shells_ - _Plastic Bottles_ - _Prunings_ (sharp) - _Quack Grass_ - _Quassia Tree Shavings_ - _Radishes_ - _Red Bush Tea_ - _Rosemary Sprigs_ - _Sacrificial Plantings_ - _Sage Brush_ - _Salt Rings_ - _Sand_ - _Sandpaper_ - _Scratchy Stuff_ - _Seaweed_ - _Ssukcha_ - _Sweet Gum Tree pods_ - _Sweet Woodruff_ - _Swiss Chard_ (red-leaved) - _Talcum Powder_ - _Vermiculite_ - _WD-40_ - _Wormwood Tea_.

Beer Batter

Take a couple of tablespoons of flour and keep adding a little beer at a time until the mixture becomes smooth. This is your beer batter, and you can use just a teaspoon of this as bait within a paper cup turned on its side.

Place several of these cups around your garden to attract the beer-loving slug, or use on successive nights. In the morning you should be pleased to find a cup full of slugs which have become trapped by the floury mixture and died. Dispose of each cup to decompose with the slugs in your compost bin.

Beer Trap, or *'Slug Pub'*

Slugs love the fermentation gases which emanate from beer. Why not give them a bit of what they love? Bury a container such as an old margarine pot in the ground, so that the lip stands about 1" (2.54cm) proud. This should prevent other, more beneficial, creatures from accidentally falling in.

Then fill at least half full with (preferably) stale beer. It would be a shame to give slugs the really good stuff, and they aren't connoisseurs - although they are known to have their favorites! Greasing, or soaping, the container on the inside helps to prevent any slugs which haven't become anesthetized by the beer and drowned from making their drunken escape.

Leave the beer trap overnight and wait for it to fill up with inebriated, drowning, slugs. This is an excellent method of slug disposal, as they can then be carefully removed and deposited in your compost bin to decompose and become plant food. The ultimate plant revenge!

Incidentally, your choice of beer really could make a difference. A study was undertaken by Professor Whitney Cranshaw of Colorado State University to discover this very important element of slug control. The fascinating results show a slug preference for Kingsbury Malt Beverage, with Michelob and Budweiser not far behind. However, no comparison was made with British beers or other worldwide beverages, although Guinness is known to be a slug favorite. In general, the yeastier the beer the better.

Of course, a better use of beer would be to drink it yourself and then stagger round the garden in the dark with a torch, gate-crash the evening slug banquet and just pick them up yourself. Then dispose of them using one of the methods described in *Disposal of Slugs*.

(As alternatives, also see *Grape Juice*, and *Yeast*).

Note: It is not a good idea to use any of the Beer Trap methods if you are also actively encouraging natural predators such as frogs, lizards and newts, as they may well suffer the same fate as the slugs. One way of discouraging these predators from the beer trap is to ensure that access is quite difficult. As we know, it is difficult to keep slugs out of even the tightest spots.

Beetles

Ground beetles, particularly varieties of the carabid beetle, can be voracious slug eaters. Although they may also eat earthworms, they do not harm your garden in general, so are to be strongly encouraged if you have a slug problem.

This may be difficult, other than providing a habitat which they will enjoy - in common with amphibians, as well as hedgehogs, you can't go far wrong with a pile of logs, leaves or stones - but the main message is not to discourage any ground beetles which you may come across. Not all will eat slugs, but the chances are that they will do a good job for you.

Examples of these types of beetle are:

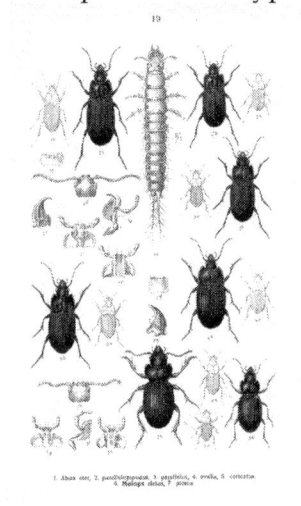

Abax Parallelepipedus Beetles

These ground beetles are native to Europe, primarily, and you will be delighted to learn that slugs are its main prey. They are particularly partial to the Arion hortensis (the black field slug, or garden slug), but will also go for snails at a pinch, as well as other pests such as the sawfly. As they cause no harm to plants themselves they are the ideal garden ally.

Violet Ground Beetles (also known as the *Rain Beetle*)

Being nocturnal, you may not see the Violet Ground Beetle very often, but the clue can be found in the alternative common name, rain beetle, which 'feeds at night, likes the rain'. Sound familiar? Incidentally, the liking for rain is primarily because evolution has taught them that this is a good time to find its favorite prey, the slug! As an added bonus, violet ground beetles also enjoy vine weevils, another enemy of the gardener.

Finally, the _Rove Beetle_ has a widely varied diet which may include slugs, so you can add those to your list of beneficial insects.

Bin Liner

Your black bin liner can also be used as a slug trap. Lay this down in between your plants and prop open the opening with two old lettuce heads to attract the slugs. Sprinkle or spray them with beer to draw the slugs in, and away from your other plants. In the morning check the bag and you should find that the feasted slugs have decided to remain there for shelter until the next evening feed. This need never happen - remove the slugs to your destination of choice, and re-set the trap the following evening.

Birds
Blackbirds, Crows, Fieldfare, Grackles, Gulls, Jackdaws, Jays, Magpies, Owls, Pigeons, Ravens, Redwings, Robins, Rooks, Starlings, and Thrushes are all known to enjoy as many slugs or snails as they can find.

Thrushes are renowned for being particularly partial to snails, for example, and an easy way to monitor your success in attracting a thrush population will be the amount of broken snail shells you may find in your garden. The thrush has evolved to make intelligent use of a handy stone to crack the shells open.

A bird bath in your garden will be an encouragement to birds in general, as will any popular bird snack such as can be found in your local pet store. Slugs and snails will count among their most popular delicacies, so you should actively court the bird population for as long as you have these marauding mollusks in your garden. How long will that be? Realistically there will always be a supply of slugs for your garden birds to eat, but by using the methods in this book you have the means to control the situation.

Bordeaux Mixture
This amalgam of copper sulfate and a mixture of hydrated lime can be slapped onto tree trunks or really thick-stemmed plants to prevent any upward progress. This deterrent could easily be effective for an entire slug season.
(also see _Copper Sulfate_)

Bridges

This may seem obvious in hindsight, but if you are wondering why your carefully prepared barriers are not preventing slugs and snails from carrying on their marauding ways then take a look around to see what bridges they have found to afford them access.

These creatures can move around on many surfaces, in death-defying positions, so have they managed to find a bridge, or a succession of bridges somewhere to take them to their goal? Get inside a slug's mind and remove any bridges it may think of using!

Buttermilk
(see *Buttermilk Spray Recipe*)

Cabbage Trap
Boil some old cabbage leaves until they become soft, then place in your garden just before dusk in an area where you have previously observed slugs. To entice them more eagerly you can melt a little lard or margarine then disperse this over the leaves. After two or three hours put some disposable gloves on, take a torch with you, and collect your slug harvest. Dispose of them humanely.
(see *Disposal of Slugs*)

Cat Food Trap

Dry cat food is also a rare treat for slugs. Pour a handful into a corner of your garden and sprinkle with water until it becomes soft. Find an old plastic or foil dish and cut two small entrances in the side. This will be used to cover the food so that it will be a slug and snail trap rather than a feast for other wildlife.

Weigh down the covering container to prevent it blowing away or being flipped, then sit back and wait for your prey. Inspect it after a few hours or in the morning and count your catch.
(also see <u>Dog Food Trap</u>)

Cat Litter
Some brands of cat litter will contain diatomite, a substance found to be discouraging for slugs and snails to crawl over. Sprinkle some of this cat litter among your plants and you will add one extra deterrent factor between your precious plants and those ravenous mollusks.

Chicken Layers' Mash
Unless you are a chicken farmer or have laying chickens in your backyard you may not come across chicken mash very often. However, it is worth looking into, because slugs and snails are known to be attracted to it, and this lovely bait will keep them lurking around beneath your trap, ripe and ready for picking in the morning.

You can obtain chicken mash quite easily and inexpensively in pet stores or online - and you won't need a lot of it, after all. A couple of heaped teaspoons should do it, every day until your trap has served its purpose.

The advantages? It is safe for other animals to eat, unlike poisonous baits, and it should attract your massive mollusk population very quickly. If you don't wake up next morning to a lovely slug harvest beneath your trap (an upturned plant pot saucer or a piece of cardboard of a similar size, leaving a small access area) then you may not have as large a slug problem as you thought. However, you must be sure to lay the trap correctly (see _Traps_).

Chickens
Chickens love eating slugs. Keeping chickens would be a big step to take just to dispose of the slugs in your garden, but if you had a vague interest in having some laying hens beforehand then this may bring it forward as a priority. Check your local authority regulations first of course. You would want to stick to the small breeds, though, such as Rhode Island Reds, as the larger ones could cause as much havoc to your garden as slugs! You will find the Rhode Island Red a great slug scavenger. No slug nor snail will be safe!

Chipmunks
Chipmunks can't get enough snails and slugs. Whether you would want to encourage chipmunks around your land is a different matter, but if your slug and snail population has reached epic proportions then you may have reason not to actively discourage these predators, for a while at least.

Cinders
see *Ash*

Citrus
Slugs are attracted to citrus fruit, but the acidic qualities of citrus can kill them. They go for grapefruit particularly, but you could substitute with oranges or lemons.

Surround your protected area with half a grapefruit skin, preferably with some flesh remaining, inverted so that it lies face down. Slugs will inevitably be drawn to this potential death trap, and as you know, it is almost impossible to keep a slug out of anywhere. You can, of course, give them a helping hand by cutting a small hole in the side. This may be the last thing they ever do.

An alternative, if you wish to speed up the attraction process, is to add some beer in the base of a half grapefruit, to about 1" (2.54cm) depth, but this time position the fruit as a saucer. Slugs should be strongly attracted both to the beer and to the citrus, and will meet a fairly pleasant death drowning in beer.

The death trap can, of course, be reused for a while until it loses its citrus appeal, and then put in your compost, deceased mollusks and all.

Coconut Shells
Leave an upturned coconut shell, or several, in the garden at night. The moisture will entice slugs in, where you can find them hiding in the morning, ready to be disposed of elsewhere (see _Disposal of Slugs_).

Coffee
Whether you use coffee grounds or a liquid coffee solution, the caffeine can prove fatal to slugs and snails, as it apparently speeds up their heart rate to the point that they have a coronary attack. You will find that vegetarian varieties are strongly drawn to the caffeine, whereas the carnivorous types will avoid it completely and go elsewhere.

You could add some coffee grounds to some mulch which you spread around your protected areas, or simply scatter the grounds on the ground. This is a nicely organic method, which should harm nothing but the unwanted slug, but it will almost certainly slow plant growth. In the long run it may be more generally beneficial to your garden by adding nitrogen to the soil and increasing soil acidity. In fact you may have an additional benefit if unwanted cats also visit your garden, as they will tend to be repelled through their dislike of the smell of coffee.

You could also make your own caffeine spray (see *Spray Recipes*).

Try a potentially lethal cocktail of coffee grounds, eggshells and diatomaceous earth as a good mix to deter slugs and snails.

Comfrey Trap
(also see *Lettuce*)
This invasive plant is useful medicinally but you may find its best use as a slug trap. The high-protein leaves of the comfrey plant hold great appeal for slugs and snails, and you can take advantage of this to make a simple slug trap in the form of a pile of leaves in your garden where you have seen slugs previously.

They will call in en masse for a comfrey party, and when you are ready for some slug picking put on those gloves and dispose of as many as you can find (see *disposal of slugs*). After a few days you should be finding that fewer and fewer slugs are being drawn to the comfrey, so you could pick the pile up and add it to your compost bin along with any remaining slugs.

As a further precaution you could ring your garden with any remaining comfrey leaves to catch the lingering marauders, then dispose of the comfrey traps in your compost bin once again.

Commercial Slug Killers

Not dealt with in this book of more natural methods of slug control, but you can read reviews of the latest commercially available methods at our website, www. slugprevention.com.

Companion Planting

There are two ways of looking at companion planting. You could either choose to plant deterrent plants close by those which you need to protect, or you could plant sufficient crops which slugs love and will munch happily without disturbing your prized possessions.

Among the plants which are known to act as a deterrent to slugs are anise, fennel, geranium leaves, ginger, lavender, rosemary, rue (ruta), sage, sweet woodruff, Swiss chard (red-leaved), thyme, and wormwood. For examples of plants which will distract slugs see also *Crops Trap*, and *Sacrificial Planting*.

Compost Trap

A compost bin isn't a trap, strictly speaking, as slugs may be able to find their way out, but you should find that slugs will love the rotting vegetation so much that they will never leave. Carnivorous slugs less so, depending on the quantity of their chosen prey.

If you hand-pick whatever slugs you can find, create a hole in your compost and deposit the slugs within the hole before covering them up, then you should find that they will actually improve the composting process, turning any rotting vegetation into compost. As a bonus, if any animal fats end up in your compost (not generally a good idea) then slugs will also break this down for you.

However, there are two points to bear in mind with slugs in compost. Carnivorous slugs will eat any earthworms they come across within the compost - although they are likely to be already gorged on the delicious rotting material. Nevertheless, it is advisable to maintain a strong earthworm bias.

You should also be sure to position your compost away from any tasty plants which may encourage your compost slugs to leave their cosy, decaying, home. You can of course discourage this by surrounding your compost bin with some of the many slug barriers to choose from, such as egg shells, oak bark, sharp gravel, sand, etc.

Copper

Copper is quite well known as a slug deterrent. From the slug's point of view, copper acts as a catalyst with its slime to cause a temporary breakdown in its nervous system, so for potted plants which particularly attract slugs you should find that a wide copper barrier around the pot will do the trick. You can create a copper barrier to forestall sluggy access to any of your plants - or indeed your home - to stem the flow of those unwanted invaders. Copper strips are widely available, but in my experience it is not a great challenge for a slug to span across most of these strips without touching them. For this reason, I recommend using a double strip, extending the barrier to 3 inches (7.62cm) or more. The more the better, of course. If you need really strong protection a 6-inch (15.24cm) deep copper barrier, buried to a depth of 2 inches (5.08cm) is a daunting challenge for any slug, according to research by the University of California. Even the largest of slugs would have difficulty in bridging such an obstacle, and of course the electro-magnetic reaction would cause a strong deterrent. When dealing with copper you should be aware that it will tarnish quite swiftly, and regular cleaning with vinegar is necessary to maintain its effectiveness. If you can't afford copper tape, or prefer a home-made solution, then simply saving up your copper pennies and overlaying them around any vulnerable plants may provide some defense, as long as the copper is not tarnished (first clean with vinegar) and the breadth is insurmountable for your garden's size of slug. Another tip for the impecunious or avid recycler is to extract the copper strands from your everyday scouring pads. You would be surprised at the length of these strands, and as long as you don't need to protect a large area against slugs then you can wind and weave to your heart's content.

Copper Sulfate
An easier - though less permanent - alternative to copper would be some deft spraying of copper sulfate in a light pattern around areas of slug or snail infestation. This won't last for very long, particularly following rain, so be prepared for repeated spraying over a short period of time (see *Note*).

Be warned, however, that some slug species are barely bothered by copper sulfate, so it is recommended to try this relatively quick solution first before embarking on more labor-intensive methods. You should be able to pick up some copper sulfate in your local pharmacy or chemist, depending on where you live.

You may also try a richer concentration of copper sulfate to coat tree trunks in a similar way to <u>Bordeaux mixture</u>. This is unlikely to prove to be as effective or long-lasting, but avoids the need to create your own mixture.

Note: Copper sulfate is a chemical compound, and will have a derogatory effect on the soil in the long run, being particularly detrimental to the worm population. Be sure to thoroughly read and adhere to the instructions on the label.

Cornmeal

Try sprinkling a good quantity of cornmeal around your most prized plants. Slugs should go for the cornmeal first, and if they eat enough of it they become bloated and die, or at the very least find it difficult to move easily and become easy pickings for predators or a gloved hand.

Cotton Wool

Tie some pieces of cotton wool around the stem of your most prized or vulnerable plants and this will deter slugs and snails from gaining access to munch at the leaves.

Crops Trap

You could use a variety of crops to attract and gather those marauding slugs in a single place so that you can deal with them all at once. Try these favorites first if you can source them: lettuce, marigolds, plantain, zinnias, comfrey leaves, and you could also try beans.

Cultural Control

What is a slug's preferred habitat? Damp, shady areas with decaying vegetation. What would deter slugs from choosing your garden to live in and feed on your plants? Simple. The removal of areas which would appeal to a slug.

So this means opening your garden up to the sun as much as possible, clearing dying or decaying material from any sheltered corners where slugs may snooze during the day and monitoring any moist areas where slugs will lay their eggs. There is little point in eradicating slugs from your garden if the next generation are lurking beneath the soil.

Daddy Longlegs (NOT the *Crane Fly*)
(see *Harvestmen*)

Decollate Snails
Not only will these small, carnivorous snails eat other slugs and snails in your garden but they should leave all but your youngest plants alone as well. A perfect example of man and mollusk living in harmony. This sounds too good to be true, so what is the catch with this attractive snail?

Well, first of all you should check whether their importation into your state or country is legal. Several of the United States will restrict them, as they are deemed to be an invasive species, which thrives in a warm climate.

Secondly, you should not use any of the slug eradication methods referred to in this book while the decollate snail population establish themselves, as none of these methods are likely to differentiate between the type of slug or snail. However, any form of non-deadly slug trap described within these pages will only serve to trap slugs along with the carnivorous snail, which can only be bad news for the slug.

Deterrents
see *Barriers, Companion Planting, Sacrificial Planting*

Diatomaceous Earth
Spread diatomaceous earth around your plants and this will deter slugs from challenging its texture. The abrasive nature of diatomaceous earth can cut their skin, ultimately resulting in dehydration and death. Unfortunately the dusty properties of this fossilized earth make it rather unpleasant to deal with, and it is likely to require regular reapplication, particularly following rain or high winds.

Disposal of Slugs
So now you have some slugs under your control, what do you do with them?

Dead
Compost bin (but don't overdo it, because dead slugs or snails will tend to rot like meat; they are protein-rich however, and once composted they will be beneficial to the soil).
Alive

- Compost bin (in moderation, as long as there is no easy escape). Surround the compost with one of the barriers referred to in this book as prevention; as mentioned earlier, slugs are very efficient at recycling organic matter; adult slugs, in particular, actually prefer rotting old stuff and many will also eat any dead slugs or animal fats which are in there, turning it all nicely into rich compost)
- Freezer

  This may sound quite cruel, and of course no-one can really say for sure, but putting any slugs you have caught in the freezer is apparently a relatively humane way of dispatching them. The squashing method is pretty unappealing, if quick, and can also leave rather a mess, so slowing down the cold-blooded slug's metabolism in the freezer as they die could be considered a form of anaesthesia. Be sure to place the slugs in a rigid container with a lid, however, because a flimsy plastic bag may not be sufficient to contain a quantity of muscular slugs.
- Leave vulnerable to predators, surrounded by slug-resistant barriers.

Dog Food Trap

Dry dog food isn't just for dogs. Slugs love it too! Simply deposit a pile in an area where they regularly gather, moisten with a little water to soften it, then cover with an inverted foil or plastic container with inviting entry holes cut into the sides.

Place a stone or rock on top to weigh it down so it would be difficult for other wildlife to flip it over and gain access, then await the slug reaction. This may take a couple of hours, depending on the time or dampness of the day, but you should soon find a nice collection of slugs to dispose of. You could leave this overnight if you wish and inspect it in the morning. (also see *Cat Food Trap*)

Dry Surfaces

Slugs find it difficult to secrete enough mucus to move over very dry surfaces, such as cinders, flour, gravel, sand, sawdust, or talcum powder and will generally avoid these areas. They can get across any dry, or dusty surface, just like you can walk across gravel in bare feet, but they will prefer not to. They can get across most scratchy surfaces too, just like you could walk over broken glass in bare feet, but would you really want to?

Ducks

Have you ever considered the benefits of a pet duck living in your garden? You will enjoy the eggs, of course, but you will also enjoy the lack of slugs. Most ducks will eat pretty much anything, so naturally you would need to protect vulnerable young plants with some netting. Fortunately, slugs and snails are among their favorites. Which breeds of duck would you particularly benefit from? Depending on where you live, domestic ducks such as Indian runners or Khaki Campbells should be ideal, as would the Mallard, a wild duck which may come and go but would return if the arrangement is beneficial.

Epsom Salts

You should receive a double benefit from this measure, as not only will Epsom Salts deter slugs from any area where it has been sprinkled, but in addition the magnesium contained within the salts will correct any magnesium deficiency from which your plants may be suffering. As you may know, plants respond to magnesium by building up their roots while also thickening and enriching the color of their petals.

Flour

Pour quantities of this around your plants and slugs will have difficulty in crossing the dry surface and hopefully turn to a sacrificial planting (see dry surfaces; sacrificial planting).

Fly Screen Barrier

You could try this ingenious method by positioning a mesh fly screen outside a frame encircling your precious plants, embedded in the soil. As long as the screen rises at least 4 inches (10.16cm) above the surface then you have created an effective barrier against the slug.

You could also use the pop-up tent type of mesh fly screen (such as may be used to cover cakes), positioned above young plants which are less than 12 inches (30cm) or so tall. As with many other types of barrier, however, your garden will be less attractive for it.

Foxes

Slugs form a small part of a fox's diet. They know where to look for them and will hunt down the slimies while you sleep. But, as you must have a slug problem to be reading this, it is likely that you don't have many foxes in the vicinity. Most people would prefer to discourage foxes in the proximity of their gardens of course.

However, if you should be one of those folk who enjoy fox-watching - or you prefer foxes to slugs - then if at dusk you regularly collect together a distribution of slugs throughout your garden into one easy-access spot (hemmed in by slug-resistant boundaries) then the fox, among many other slug eaters, will see to it that they won't be there on the following morning.

Frogs
see *Toads*

Fruit Skins

Eat your healthy breakfast of grapefruit, have an orange for lunch, a melon in the evening, then retain the skins to place in the garden during the early evening. Make sure they are close to your enemy's favorite eating places, and leave them there on the soil, skin side down. After breakfast next day go out to inspect your catch. You are very likely to find that a proportion of your slug population has decided the nice, moist, inviting space inside of the fruit's peel is just the place for a nap after the evening's indulgence.

If you are lucky you may be able to pick the fruit skins up and deposit the slugs into your lethal bucket of salty water. Alternatively, wear a pair of disposable gloves and pick out any slugs by hand to drop into the bucket of doom.

Fur
see *Hair*

Garden Management
see *Cultural Control*

Garlic

Here is a delicious garlic recipe for snails (and slugs). No, it's not what you think! Take two full bulbs of garlic, crush them until they are becoming pulp, then blanch them briefly in boiling water, using one pint (0.47 liters) per bulb. Around four minutes should do it, just sufficient for softening.

Top up to the original amount of liquid (one pint per bulb). Once cooled, you have a pungent mixture to deter slugs and snails from your precious plants.

This gastronomic concoction is so unpleasant to the gastropod's sense of smell that you only need to use a small amount at a time, approximately one tablespoon to one gallon (3.785 liters) of water dispensed to the leaves and stems of your plants. Reapply every week or two, or more frequently following rainfall.

Used as a spray, this garlic concoction should also kill any slugs which are sprayed upon. Further strengthen with garlic as required.

You could also try adding some chili, vegetable oil and soap to increase its effectiveness against resistant slugs.

Geranium Leaves

Slugs don't enjoy hairy plants such as geraniums, and their aroma also puts them off, so their leaves can form a good barrier to protect your more appetizing plants. Some types of slug will navigate their way through a simple geranium barrier if the prize is worth getting, however, so it is best to use this in conjunction with other barrier materials referred to elsewhere.

Incidentally, if you want some worry-free color for your garden then the slug-resistant geranium is a good choice. The more you fill your garden with slug-resistant plants (geraniums, begonias, borage/starflowers, fuchsias, impatiens, lantana, nasturtiums, poppies, as well as aromatic plants such as ginger, lavender, oregano, rosemary, sage and thyme), the less attractive it will be to the invading slug. You could also position these around the more delicate plants in your garden.

Ginger
Powdered ginger can form a useful barrier against slug intrusion, particularly as an ingredient in harmony with some of the other barrier materials referenced elsewhere in this book. It's always worth keeping a supply of powdered ginger in your kitchen, whether you cook with it or not.

Grackles
Voracious slug-eating birds for readers in the Americas to encourage. If you see grackles in your neighborhood then try scattering some seed in your garden regularly, as grackles prefer to eat from the ground. Any nearby slugs will stand no chance. They will even turn over objects in their search for food, so there is no place to hide. Bear in mind, however, that grackles will also eat any insect they come across, which would be bad news for the beneficial insects in your garden.

Grape Juice Trap
An alternative to the beer trap. If you can't be bothered with constructing a trap as described in the Beer Trap section, nor want to waste good beer, then an easier option is to put the grape juice in a saucer, or preferably something a little deeper, and leave overnight in your garden. You could well be disposing of a drowned slug or two in the morning. Slugs aren't particularly discriminating when it comes to grape juice, so don't waste your money on the good stuff, unless you want to drink some yourself.

Grapefruit
see *Citrus*

Grease
Slugs can't really cope with grease, so this will form an effective barrier to prevent them from climbing up, or over, anything you wish to protect. Use in combination with sand and you have real slug protection. As mentioned with other barriers of this type, you should spread at least three inches of a barrier material to prevent the larger slugs from looping over the whole thing. You have to admire them really, and give them some grudging respect!

Ground Beetles
These little insects are voracious eaters for their size, and are generally beneficial to your garden. Of particular interest to us here, though, is the quantity of slugs they will munch their way through given half a chance. They will hunt them down incessantly. They may not be particularly apparent as they go about their work for you, as most of them are more active during the night - as, fortunately, is your average slug - and they also prefer to go about their business under cover.

This means, of course, that it may be difficult to gauge your success in attracting them. However, you can try to encourage them into your garden by building up a log pile, or a mound of stones, which they will make use of for nesting in the summer and also settle down within for the winter.

During the autumn and winter they will be much less active, if at all, so they are not a year-round solution. In spring, however, they will be incredibly active in hunting out young slugs, as well as slug eggs, which should greatly diminish the slug stock for the next few months.

Hair

Hair today, gone tomorrow. Simply surround your prized plants with a generous helping of hair or fur (thick human hair or horse hair works best) and slugs will have a difficult time traversing the barrier. Better still, they are pretty likely to tangle themselves up in hair and strangle themselves in the process. As an added bonus the decomposing hair will add nitrogen to the soil beneath. Hairdressers should be delighted if you were to collect hair trimmings from them on a regular basis.

Hand Picking

You are likely to find the greatest amount of slugs by rampaging through your garden within two or three hours of the sun setting, particularly after rain. Step out quietly, and listen out for the munching, slurping, sound of the feasting fiends! Then turn on your torch and be prepared for some serious hand picking. Gloves are optional.

As for disposal, there are several more humane methods which are preferable to some of the sadistic ways which you may have read about. What goes around comes around I say. A handy bucket of salted, or soapy, water should do the trick, but if you are the type who prefers not to invite bad karma then you could simply place them in a large container with a lid. If you live close to some open woodland, away from houses or farms, then you could do worse than to re-home your slug population as far away from yourself and other people as possible.

Harvestmen

Harvestmen are natural predators of slugs. They do also include plant material in their omnivorous diet, but in general you can assume that your slimy friend will cause far more havoc. Their habitat is quite similar to a slug's in some ways, preferring damp areas and you could well find them near grass and leaf compost. Many of them are active at night, a good time for slug hunting.

Harvestmen can sometimes be confused with craneflies, and also the long-legged cellar spider, neither of which are recognized as slug predators, although there could be exceptions.

Hedgehogs
One of the great slug-eaters, you can encourage a hedgehog to take up residence in your garden by providing a cosy home comprising a pile of logs. If you already have a nice thick hedge for it to live in, all the better.

You could also consider constructing hedgehog nest boxes. Make them about one-and-a-half feet (45.72cm) square in size, buried in the soil or a mound of leaf mold. Provide an entrance tunnel and add some form of ventilation, such as a pipe just above the ground. A perfect, safe hibernation hideaway, ready to emerge from in the spring.

Hedgehogs should be attracted to your garden quite readily if it is currently a slug paradise, although it is quite possible that you will never know if a hedgehog is there, being shy, nocturnal animals. If you do see one during the day time then it may be in distress as they normally prefer not to make their presence known.

However, do bear in mind that this book is all about slug control using as many natural methods as possible, but we should not wish to eradicate a valuable food source for many creatures, including the hedgehog. Using chemical poisons to kill slugs will, of course, have a pretty detrimental effect on scavengers.

Herbs
Lavender, *Mint*, *Rosemary* and *Sage* are particularly aromatic from a slug perspective. What is one of the few things they reject? Aromatic herbs. Either sprinkle the leaves around areas which you want to protect, or grow the herbs in suitable places to form an appropriate barrier.

Hiding Places (also see _Cultural Control_)
There are specific places where slugs like to lurk. Remove these places from your garden and you will have removed part of the problem right away. So as a first step, take away as many weeds, rocks, wood and general debris as you can. Anywhere which is damp and shady. OK, so this may be counter-productive to some of the predator-encouraging ploys referred to elsewhere in this book, and it can be worthwhile leaving just one designated hiding place area (see _Know Where They Are_).

Horseradish

Horseradish leaves and roots act as good slug deterrents. You could pile these up in the garden, along with an amount of grapefruit halves, as well as comfrey perhaps. Then pick the whole mount up once a week, chuck it into some soapy water for an hour, then dispose of the whole lot in your compost. Another use for the horseradish root is to incorporate it into a slug-ridding spray (see *Spray Recipes*).

Hostas

If you want to grow hostas, one of the choicest delicacies for slugs, then you would be well advised to avoid their known favorites (e.g. those with white and green leaves), and choose the slug's least-favored varieties. In general, these are the varieties with thick and heavily textured leaves, or with blue leaves, which are more resistant to slugs, though not immune of course. Examples of these varieties include most of the blue varieties, such as Blue Angel and Blue Ice, also Elegans, Halycon, Invincible, Sagae, and the Sum and Substance family, amongst too many others to list here, this not being a book about hostas.

Of course you can try any of the slug barriers referred to in this book against these and the less resistant varieties, and slug traps would be well-placed close to your hostas. That is where slugs are highly likely to be found, but your trap would need to be more enticing than the hostas themselves.

Another idea would be to plant one or two of the favored varieties as sacrificial hostas for slugs to attack in a remote part of your garden. Add some wild violets to the mix and you can create a slug haven. Then fiercely protect all your other plantings and keep the slugs distracted elsewhere.

Insects
Lightning Bugs (Fireflies, Glowworms), *Marsh Flies*

Isopropyl Alcohol
Mix up a spray comprising one part isopropyl alcohol with eight parts water, then spray directly on slugs, taking care to avoid contact with your plants. This will dry the slug up, and is somewhat akin to the salt method, which I don't recommend either. This is strictly a last-ditch effort if all else fails.

Know Where They Are!
Knowing where the slugs in your garden are lurking is half the battle. We know where slugs like to hide during the daytime. So create these lairs for them, then you will know where to find them. Out-thinking slugs isn't a difficult proposition, and the best advice is always to know your 'enemy's' habits.

The best location to choose would be in the dampest place in your garden (which will also attract some natural predators of slugs, such as frogs, toads and newts), where you can set up a series of slug stopovers. Good materials for this are wood offcuts, cardboard, pieces of old carpet, or broken slates.

Turn these over regularly, preferably first thing in the morning, and you should find a significant slice of your slug population beneath. See *Disposal of Slugs* for what to do next.

Lava Rock

You can buy lava rock for your outdoor grill, or you can buy it for your garden protection. Slugs avoid abrasive surfaces so will be inclined to leave alone any plant within the barrier. Regularly inspect the barrier for garden debris which will allow slugs an easy passageway through to the plant.

Lavender

A slug deterrent, which you can spread thickly around prized plants as a barrier. You can also use rosemary sprigs which, like lavender, have a strong scent which slugs dislike.

Leopard Slugs

Leopard slugs are light grey in color, measuring up to 8 inches (20.32cm), recognizable by the patterned black spots across its back, sometimes resembling leopard or tiger stripes.

This method is a moot point, and depends very much upon where you live. The leopard slug is indigenous to Europe, but has since spread to most other regions of the world. In the United States it is present in 46 states, and also 5 of 10 provinces in Canada, as well as in Mexico and parts of South America. Because it will eat young crops at a voracious pace, faster than the crops can grow, they are listed as a major pest in those 46 states. However, if you live in other regions, far from agricultural land and you have a slug problem, you could find the leopard slug to be your friend, as it will eat other slugs and snails, as well as ridding your garden of decaying vegetable matter, fungi and algae. The leopard slug will generally prefer this high protein diet to eating your vegetation, and it is the Usain Bolt of the slug world. So as long as you have just the one 'Usain Bolt', or maybe a relative or two, then rather than being a pest they should reduce the overall slug population.

You could also use dispose of any dead slugs by strewing them around the base of your plants. Any leopard slugs in the neighborhood will gorge on these and consequently be much less likely to go on to attack your valued vegetation.

Lettuce
(also see *Comfrey*)
You could choose to grow plenty of lettuce around your more prized crops to form a 'sacrificial barrier' as the first staging post for any marauding slugs. They will gorge on lettuce and tend not to move on.

As a bonus, once the slugs have finished munching away on the lettuce leaves they are then likely to rest up for the day within their folds, and will be easy to pick off whenever you inspect any damage from the previous night's feeding fest.

Marigolds are also useful as sacrificial plantings, and as a double barrier they would not only help in hiding the less attractive lettuce from view but protect your valued plants twice over.

Should you actually want to grow lettuce to eat rather than as a sacrifice then may I recommend the red oak leaf lettuce, which is not only rather tasty but is also likely to be left alone by slugs.

Light

Once a slug has set up home inside your home it can be very difficult to track it down. It will find a very, very small hiding place during the day and come out again at night.

As a temporary solution to having to deal with slimy trails around the house when you get up in the morning, leave the light on overnight in the affected area. Obviously a low wattage eco bulb is best for this. In the meantime you can try one of the slug-hunting methods (see *Slugs in the House*) at a time of your choosing.

Lightning Bugs (or *Fireflies*)
The larvae of lightning bugs (aka *glowworms*) devour whatever slugs, snails, and their eggs that they can find when they emerge in the spring. This period of voracious eating will last for several weeks, prior to pupation.

It won't be easy to attract lightning bugs into your garden habitat, but if you have a pond then you will be stacking the odds in your favor. One of the reasons lightning bugs tend to live close to water is precisely because those are the same conditions that attract their larvae's prey, slugs and snails among them. An alternative to having a pond would be a damp area of your garden, allowing a few weeds to linger there.

It is also known that lightning bugs like living near long grass, which conceals them better during the day and allows them a high point to display from at night. As you probably won't want your grass to be as long as a firefly would prefer, a suitable compromise would be keeping any grass close to your pond a little longer, and not over-mowing your lawn in general, at least while your slug population is higher than you would like.

Lime
Sprinkle a line of agricultural lime, ground limestone or powdered chalk around lime-loving plants to deter slugs, as the effort it takes to produce a slime trail across such dry, dusty surfaces as lime will encourage them to slime elsewhere, perhaps towards a sacrificial area - if you have had the foresight to plant suitable sacrifices.

Hydrated lime (calcium hydroxide), also known as slaked, or builders' lime, can be spread on your soil close to known slug habitats, although obviously not close to plants requiring an acidic soil.

If you combine hydrated lime with copper sulfate to make Bordeaux mixture and paint this on plants such as grape vines, tree trunks or any other surface where snails or slugs are found then you won't find them there anymore. Although it is widely approved for organic use, you shouldn't overuse this mixture close to the soil, however, as it can be harmful to earthworms, nor should it be applied close to fish or livestock.

Lint

You can make good use of the lint produced by tumble dryers as a slug barrier. Slugs are unable to slime across the fiber in the lint. However, fabric softener used during washing will leave some chemical residue in the lint, so this is not a good long-term solution.

If you really want to give it a try though, you could experiment with adding three or four ounces (88-118ml) of white vinegar as a substitute for fabric softener, evaporating during the final rinse to leave the clothes odor-free and static-free.

This is not an explicit recommendation - you are advised to try this with your less treasured items of clothing first, so that you will gain experience in using the correct amount.

Lizards
Natural predators of slugs, which you could encourage into your garden by offering some shelter among a pile of rocks in a quiet area. Different species of lizards tend to be found almost anywhere in the world so the chances are that you have plenty of them nearby which will gladly help you out with your slug problem if you help them out with a safe habitat.

Marigolds
Can be used as _sacrificial plantings_.
(also see _Lettuce_).

Marsh Flies
A real enemy of the slug, as their parasitic larvae will burrow into them and kill up to two dozen before emerging as flies. It's obvious by their name that marsh flies are commonly found in a damp environment, another good reason for having a garden pond, with plenty of wild flowers close by.

Another name for marsh flies is snail-killing flies, which emphasizes their nature. A female marsh fly can lay up to 300 eggs, so that adds up to a lot of dead slugs and snails. As their most significant parasite, the appearance of marsh flies in their habitat spells a death sentence for slugs. They look fairly insignificant, yellowish or brown in color, measuring about one quarter inch (6mm) long, and can be hard to identify, but a trademark posture is to rest on vegetation with their head pointing at the ground.

Melon Rind
Leave your cast-off melon rinds, positioned with the skin side up, in your garden overnight, preferably close to your compost bin, and dispose of the resting, over-fed slugs and melon rind in the morning. If you can't bear to touch them, even with gloves on, then flip the rinds over so that the slugs are exposed to any onlooking birds.

Milk Trap
Use milk in the same way as for a *Beer Trap*. Slugs enjoy milk, although beer has the edge. However, if you are aware that hedgehogs frequent your garden - and eating your slugs at the same time, of course - then avoid the milk trap, as it will make hedgehogs ill if they drink it. Of course, you may not be aware of local hedgehogs, since they emerge at night, and for this reason I would recommend the beer option, or at the very least providing plenty of water close to the milk as an alternative for the hedgehog to drink.

Moles
Slug predators which you will probably prefer not to encourage into your garden if you have a lawn to protect.

Mulch
Using mulch to benefit your garden soil can be turned to even greater advantage by formulating it to discourage slugs. Regular mulch gives slugs a hiding place, especially if more than 3 inches (7.62cm) deep, but will be less likely to appeal to them if you use a variety of these mulches:

- Adding *pine needles* or *cedar chips* to your mulch, close to acid-loving plants, will increase the acidity in the soil which has the benefit of discouraging slugs from frequenting the area, also being deterred by the abrasive nature of the mulch.
- Liberally add *pecan hulls* above your mulch, increasing the concentration immediately below the bottom of the plant or where the leaves spread close to the ground. The sharp edges will deter slugs and snails, which risk cutting themselves if they try to make their way across, and an additional benefit is to increase the pH in soil low in acid.
- Try *seaweed* mulch if you are fortunate enough to have ready access. The saltiness and roughness of the seaweed will keep slugs away, although it soon becomes pretty pungent. Seaweed is an excellent fertilizer for your soil, so you could pile it up to a depth of 3 or 4 inches (7 - 10cm) before it reduces as it dries, although you should keep it from touching the plants themselves.
- Adding deterrent _herbs_ to your mulch will have a discouraging effect. *Mint*, *sage*, or *wormwood* should work, or consider using any of the deterrents listed under _Plants That Slugs Dislike_.
- Oak leaf mulch should deter slugs with its acidity.
- Quack grass can be fatal for slugs, and a quantity of chopped quack grass added to your mulch should do the trick.

- Coffee grounds as a light mulch around your plants will probably slow plant growth, but the caffeine acts as a slug deterrent. Although not actually harming the plant, in moderation, it is not advisable for vegetables, since you are actively seeking to promote their growth.

Remember, though, that as with all barriers, deterrent mulches around certain plants will only have the effect of turning the slug around in search of other food sources. Unless you have done some _sacrificial planting_ then you will be sacrificing some other beloved plant which has not been sufficiently protected.

Mullein Leaves
These are the leaves from verbascum, or velvet plant, which are used in herbal medicine. Also a slug deterrent, you can try using these either fresh or dried as a barrier around your plants. As verbascum is an attractive plant which grows up to 10 feet (3 meters) tall you could do worse than growing it around the perimeter of your property. The thick stem is also considered to be one of the best drills for friction fire lighting using the hand drill method, should you ever have the need.

Natural Slug Killers
see *Beer Batter, Beer Trap, Buttermilk Spray, Cabbage, Chicken Layers' Mash, Citrus, Comfrey, Crops, Garlic, Grape Juice, Melon Rind, Oat Bran* or small Bran Flakes, *Orange Peel, Predators, Quassia Tree Shavings, Soapy Water, Sugar Shacks, Vinegar, Wormwood Tea,* and *Yeast* for more information on how to use these resources to guide slugs towards their doom.

Neem Oil
Derived from the fruit and seeds of the neem tree, this organic pest control may help to deter slugs and snails, although its predominant use is to repel insect pests. Of course it will also be harmful to beneficial insects, such as bees and butterflies, so I would recommend its use at dusk when slugs are more likely to come out and beneficial insects less likely to get in harm's way. It doesn't smell great (an understatement), and is just as likely to repel you as much as your mollusc friends, but it is worth a try for not much outlay, then monitor the results.

Nematode Worms (*Phasmarhabditis hermaphrodita*)
As long as your soil isn't too heavy, this is a very effective method against slugs primarily, not snails. You can buy these tiny parasitical worms at garden centers, although they are not allowed in the U.S.A. at the time of writing, primarily, I believe, because they are not native species. The phasmarhabditis hermaphrodita is, however, not harmful to humans or other garden wildlife, and slugs will be their target.

However, no matter how much you may dislike your slug population you must surely have sympathy for what the predatory nematode has in store for them, so it is your choice whether or not you want to inflict a slow death of seven or more days on the poor slug. Possibly one of the few slug killers worse than salt.

You spray the worms on the ground in a solution of water, and these microscopic organisms will burrow underground to find slugs living there and lay their eggs in them. This is not a pleasant prospect, but it will be very effective.

It may take three or four days before their work starts to take effect, the slug becoming bloated and unable to feed because of bacteria introduced by the worms. This in itself will probably kill them before the eggs hatch out and the nematode feeding frenzy begins.

If necessary, you can then repeat the process on your soil about every six weeks, although you may not need to. The supply is self-replenishing, as new worms will emerge from the bodies of their hosts. Nematodes are also available by mail order, but be warned - they are not to be used in the USA, so check with your local regulations before ordering any. The mail order company should be able to advise you of the latest regulations, which will vary from time to time and from state to state.

Newts

If you have a severe slug problem then install a pond - or as an easier alternative you could simply dig a hole for a large washing-up bowl - in your garden to attract newts, along with toads and other slug predators. As long as you don't add any predatory fish to the pond, and provide some surrounding shelter for the newts then you should notice a significant reduction in the slug population.

Oak Leaves

Slugs and snails have a remarkably strong sense of smell, through their two shorter pairs of tentacles, and they are sensitive to the smell of oak leaves. Pile several of these around your prized plants and the aroma will act as a deterrent. You could also use the mulch from rotting oak leaves for the same purpose.

Oat Bran

Slugs are likely to eat oat bran and small bran flakes until it kills them, or at the very least reduces their appetite, in similar fashion to cornmeal, so sprinkle some liberally in your garden near the slug zone, making sure there is sufficient concentration for a slug to be able to have a really good feed. This will of course need to be replaced after rainfall.

Orange Peel
Attractive to slugs, you can deposit a pile of peel quite close to your compost bin, along with other citrus fruit peel and potato peelings. The best time is towards dusk, so leave these overnight and come back early in the morning. You should find quite a gathering of slugs sleeping it off beneath the peel, so you can easily scoop the whole lot up and deposit in your compost bin.

Owls
Natural predators of slugs. Placing a nest box for owls in or close to your garden will go a long way towards controlling the slug population, in addition to any unwanted rodents.

Petroleum Jelly Traps
Bury a large, deep plastic container or similar in the soil close to your plants, standing about 1 inch (2.54cm) proud of the earth so that other creatures are less likely to fall in accidentally. A slug will, of course, easily be able to surmount this barrier. Liberally coat the sides of the container with petroleum jelly to prevent the slugs climbing out.

Finally, add something which will attract slugs to the bottom. It could be grapefruit or orange peel, melon rind, lettuce, cabbage, turnips, potato peel or sliced potatoes, comfrey, milk, or beer. Pick out the slugs in the morning, or remove their hiding places and leave them for the birds.

You can also liberally coat the base and the rims of your potted plants with petroleum jelly, to deter slugs from attempting to cross the barrier. You could also mix some other deterrents into the jelly, such as salt or ginger.

Pine Needles
These give off an unpleasant aroma to slugs and snails, acting as a pungent deterrent.

Pistachio Shells
Leftover pistachio shells will not only have a residue of salt lingering amongst them but they are also sharp enough to deter most slugs. Surround whatever you wish to protect with as large a heap as you can get hold of.

Plant Covers
(see *Fly Screen Barrier*; *Plastic Bottles*)

Plants That Slugs Dislike
Depending on where you live there are no guarantees that the following plants will be entirely left alone by your garden's slug population, particularly if they are your only offerings, but as a general guide to plants and vegetables worth growing relatively safely you won't go far wrong, and a few of them will actually act as slug deterrents:

plants and shrubs
herbs and spices
****edible plants and vegetables****
Alyssum*
Artemisias*

Azaleas*
Basil***
Chard****
Chicory****
Cornflower*
Cosmos*
Daffodils*
Daylilies*
Endives****
Fennel***
Forget-Me-Not*
Foxglove*
Freesia*
Fuschia*
Garlic****
Ginger***
Grapes****
Hibiscus*
Holly*
Ivy*
Jalapeno Peppers****
Jerusalem cherry*
Kale****
Lemon balm***
Lungwort*
Mint***
Nasturtium*
Oregano***
Parsley***
Peruvian lily*
Pumpkin****
Quack grass*
Red cabbage****
Red oak leaf lettuce****

Rosemary***
Sage***
Sunflower*
Tansy*
Thyme***
Yarrow*

Plastic Bottles
This is an excellent way of recycling old plastic bottles, although it will be unsightly for prime locations in your garden. The concept is to cut the bottle open from neck to base, and then cut out strips approximately 8 inches (20.32cm) long. The width doesn't really matter as long as the curvature can mesh nicely with an adjacent strip of a similar size.

Now bury about a third of each strip's length, with the roughest edge pointing upwards, in a circular pattern to form a barrier surrounding your plants. This will deter slugs to some extent, but a further step would be to deliberately serrate the top edges by cutting small v-sections out of the plastic. If you are surrounding a large area then make sure there are no slugs trapped within the barrier.

For smaller plants, or new plantings, you could also surround the entire stem with a bottle after cutting off the top and the base. Once again, you could deliberately roughen the top edge. Not an attractive solution, but you could try the more time-consuming method of placing these cylinder barriers over the plants at dusk and removing them in the morning.

Bottle necks. You should retain the screw caps of each bottle and also 2 or 3 inches (5 - 7.5cm) of the neck. Roughen the edges if possible, then bury the top part with the screw cap in place, making sure it is firm in the soil. You will need to have enough upturned bottle tops to form a ring around the stems of plants. Now fill each to the brim with salt, making sure to keep the salt well away from the plant. This forms a barrier which slugs will be reluctant to cross.

Pond
Creating a wildlife pond, small or large, is an excellent idea for attracting the very creatures which will thrive on slugs. Frogs, toads and other amphibians will be attracted there of course, but so will numerous insects which then attract slug-eating birds such as blackbirds, grackles, thrushes and the like.

Hedgehogs will also like the type of environment which is nurtured by a wildlife pond, but be sure to leave a variety of ramps as exit points from the pond for small creatures which may accidentally fall in. You can surround the pond with a variety of colorful plants to attract plenty of insects, many of them beneficial to your garden, such as marsh flies, as well as being food for your larger good neighbors.

Potatoes
Many of the methods referred to in this book relate to above-ground plant protection, which doesn't help much with potatoes. A good starting point is to grow potatoes which are known to be more slug resistant than others. Examples, in varying degrees, are Ambo, Desiree, Lady Rosetta, Majestic, Pentland Dell, Pentland Ivory, Pentland Falcon, Record, Romano, Sante and Valor. You could also plant early-harvesting varieties, such as Heather, Kestrel or Wilja, which will have reduced exposure to slugs in the damp conditions they thrive on. These varieties should be ready for lifting in August, before the greater dampness of the fall sets in. Particularly susceptible varieties include Cara, Estima, Kingston, Marfona, and Maris Piper.

Predators
Predators of the protein-rich slug include amphibians, beetles (carnivorous ones, especially carabid beetles and other ground beetles, also rove beetles), birds (blackbirds, crows, grackles, jays, owls, certain quail (mainly the northern bobwhite), ravens, redwings, robins, seagulls, starlings, thrushes), chickens (especially Rhode Island Red), decollate snails, ducks, firebug larvae, geese, harvestmen (daddy longlegs), hedgehogs, lizards, marsh fly larvae, moles, nematodes (the phasmarhabditis hermaphrodita), opossums, raccoons, rats, salamanders, shrews, slow-worms, snakes (garden snakes also known as garter snakes, are especially beneficial), and turtles.

The types of habitat which many slug predators require are quite similar, and the best thing you can do is to leave an area to become fairly wild and undisturbed, preferably including a small pond, and wait for these natural slug predators to come to you.

Prunings
The prunings from plants with sharp thorns will act as a pretty good deterrent. Raspberries, blackberries, roses (especially Rosa Rugosa), holly, all of these would be useful as a barrier around your plants. Simply putting a collection of sharp prunings on the soil in a random fashion leaves too much to chance. They must be arranged very carefully, because we know how easily slugs can exploit a gap.

Pumice Stone
see *Lava Rock*

Quack Grass
A very useful slug deterrent, which damages a slug's nervous system, both the leaves and the roots of quack grass can either be dried, finely chopped and used as a mulch or steeped in one quart (0.95 liters) of water for 24 hours and then used as a spray on the soil. In either case, use sparingly, as it can inhibit plant growth, and be particularly careful that the spray does not come into contact with your plants, just the slugs.

Quassia Tree Shavings

You should be able to buy shavings, or powdered shavings, from the Quassia tree in health food stores, where it is sold as a herbal medicine. It will also act as a natural pesticide, not harmful to beneficial insects, but its bitterness is definitely disliked by the slug family.

It is probably best used as a spray, which is made by chopping or crushing the quassia chips and then soaking in boiling water, to a ratio of one part quassia to sixteen parts water. Once cooled and strained you can safely spray this on the soil around your plants as a slug deterrent, or on slugs themselves. They won't like it.

Radishes

Chopped radishes can act as a slug deterrent, although they may well be eaten by other creatures. It's worth experimenting with this, because they are easy and cheap to come by and some - but not all - slugs will steer clear of the radish.

Ravens

Ravens are worth attracting, large birds which will eat a substantial volume of slugs. They are quite common in areas of dense population, because of the advantages of a regular food supply. If you regularly see ravens in your locality then you may encourage them, along with other slug-eating birds by handpicking slugs and trapping them within a natural barrier, to become easy pickings.

Alternatively leave any dead slugs in a prominent place for local ravens to scavenge upon.

Red Bush Tea
(see *Rooibos*)

Redwings
Redwings, like thrushes, can eat large quantities of slugs, and will also break open a snail's shell by using a stone. It will be obvious that redwings have been at work if you regularly spot broken snail shells in your garden.

Rooibos
Otherwise known as Red Bush (translated from Afrikaans), Rooibos is a little known slug deterrent. You can buy this as Red Bush Tea, a herbal tea with a variety of health benefits. However, by sprinkling Red Bush Tea quite thickly around precious plant stems you will not only protect the plant but also be adding a useful fertilizer.

Rosemary Sprigs
Because the aroma acts as a slug deterrent you could spread plenty of rosemary sprigs as a barrier around your most precious plants. Add lavender to the mix for a double whammy.

Rove Beetles

Rove beetles, such as the Devil's Coach Horse Beetle, like to eat small slugs and slug eggs. These beetles are often black, and quite large, up to nearly 1 1/2 inches (3.81cm), but generally about a quarter that size. Look after them if they are common in your garden as they are very beneficial and won't disturb your plants. If setting beer traps always leave an inch (2.54cm) or so above the ground, as these are exactly the type of creature which may otherwise fall in and drown.

Sacrificial Planting

This method is quite simple, being a ploy to outwit the slug. We already know that types of food slugs prefer to eat, so give it to them, in quantities, so that they will head straight for your sacrificial plants, hopefully in preference to the crops or flowers which you hope they will not reach.

This distraction method is far from infallible, and will only work for a while until your sacrificial plantings have been munched through, but in the meantime you could employ some judicious hand-picking if you already know where they are likely to be.

Examples of favored plants include comfrey, lettuce, marigolds and, best of all, red clover. Although quite short-lived, and viewed by many as a weed, red clover is not only strong in propagation but rich in nitrogen and will benefit the soil as it rots down. You could also spray beer on any other nearby plants which are thought of as weeds, a sure slug magnet.

Salamanders

As with other amphibians, you will find salamanders a great slug predator to aid you in your battle. They need numerous hiding places that a pile of stones can provide, water to drink from, plenty of slugs to feed off, and they will be happy companions.

Salt

If all else fails you could protect your most valued plants with a ring of salt, at least half an inch (1.27cm) deep and three inches (7.62cm) wide. Take great care that no salt touches any plant, and that the surround is not too close to the stem. Nor will salt be good for your soil, and should definitely not be applied on a long-term basis. If it rains then it quickly soaks into the soil, and, of course, there goes your slug protection. However, you could apply it on a short-term basis in the evening during dry spells, and try to sweep the majority of it up in the morning.

An alternative method, which should keep the soil protected, is to get hold of as wide a gauge garden hose as you can find. Preferably an old one, because you will need to cut this into sections which are suitable for forming a ring around whichever area you wish to protect. Now cut off a cross section of the hose (a longitudinal slice) so that the cylinder becomes a gully, into which you can pour generous helpings of salt until it is brim full. Some slugs may manage to bridge the barrier without any salt touching them, but it will still form a strong deterrent.

Most people are aware that applying salt directly on slugs is a surefire way of killing them, but this is an unnecessarily unpleasant method of dispatching the creatures, as well as leaving a gooey mess where the slug died in agony. Slugs may not be highly sentient, but there are kinder ways of doing this. What goes around comes around…
(also see *Pistachio shells*)

Salty Water
Drowning slugs in salty water is probably only a slightly less gratuitously unpleasant method of killing slugs than pure salt. They will try to climb out of course, and it really isn't nice to have to push them back in and watch them drown in a painful environment.

Sand
Surround your plants with sand to a depth of one or two inches (2.54-5.08cm) and slugs are going to have great difficulty in crossing it. Coarse sand, such as building sand, will be more abrasive, but even soft playground sand should do the trick. The sand will become mixed with the mucus slime which aids slug movement and stick to its foot, not at all pleasant for the slug. When you become confident that your slug population is well under control - or if you have identified their favorite hiding places - you could create a sandy border about 12 inches (30.48cm) wide to deter them from getting to any your plants, although any slug eggs hatching within this boundary will regenerate the population and need to be removed once again.

Sandpaper
Cut a hole in a large piece of sandpaper and use this as a protective collar around the stems of your plants. A slit between the edge and the hole make it easier to position the collar correctly. Slugs will be very reluctant to cross it, but make sure that the diameter is wide enough to prevent slugs bridging the distance, and that low hanging leaves are well out of reach. Large orbital sander discs are worth a try, but many of them will not have a great enough diameter, unless you pack several close together.

You could also create a sandpaper effect which would look more attractive by coating surfaces such as pots or raised beds with grease and throwing sharp sand at it. This will stick to the grease, and the combination becomes a doubly difficult surface for slugs to cross.

Scratchy Stuff
If a surface cuts into a slug's soft body, composed mostly of water, then it will begin to dehydrate through dessication. Applying salt to slugs results in an extreme form of dessication, but if a slug receives little cuts from an abrasive surface then this will have a similar effect, though not so dramatic. For this reason, a scratchy surface should deter most slugs. The scratchier the better, and here are some suggestions of powerful slug deterrents: ash and cinders, diatomaceous earth, eggshells (baked then crushed), grit, lava rock, nut shells (e.g. pistachio), prunings (thorny), sharp building sand, sandpaper. You could combine as many of these as possible together, creating a really uninviting prospect.

Seaweed

If you are fortunate enough to live by the sea then there is a good chance that you could come by some seaweed. If not, refer to seaweed meal a little further on. Seaweed is a very effective slug deterrent, being both salty and coarse to move across when it dries out. It will also reduce in thickness as it becomes dry, and a healthy three or four inch (7.62 - 10.16cm) layer should shrink down by three-quarters.

However, although seaweed is beneficial for the soil, you should take great care not to let the seaweed come into contact with any of your plants. You could also use seaweed meal, which is commercially available, although in truth this is unlikely to discourage slugs very much, and certainly not remotely as effective as actual seaweed. The salt in the seaweed will repel slugs, and when it is eventually washed or dug into the soil it then becomes a great soil enhancer. Alternatively you could fertilize the soil with liquid seaweed extract.

Shrews

The common shrew includes slugs in their diet, and they aren't harmful to humans or behave as pests in general, so there should be no reason to discourage them. They prefer to live around long grass and a quiet area with plenty of hiding places to choose their nest.

Slate

A useful material for providing temporary slug accommodation. They should gather underneath after a night's feed and be ready prey for you in the morning. See also Know Where They Are.

Slow Worms

With a diet consisting entirely of small invertebrates, the slow worm, (found in Europe and parts of Asia), is one of the best slug predators that you could attract to your garden. They will tend to leave your snails alone though, but you can't have everything. Slow worms can often be found in garden compost heaps, and prefer an undisturbed habitat with long grass or well-covered areas to shield them from predators. Strangely enough, among the likely hiding places would be beneath any steel corrugated sheeting you may have lying around in the back of your garden.

Slugabed

A person who remains in bed beyond the time that people generally rise ("A lazy person who stays in bed long after the usual time for rising"). If you regularly go on a night-time slug-hunt then you may become a slugabed!

Slugs in the House!

(i) If you can identify where the slug entrance is then one of the best deterrents is to pile up a large mound of salt immediately in front of it. No slug will cross this, and would die if it tried. However, if a slug is already in the house and hiding somewhere then you will have trapped it inside. In that event you could try methods iii or iv.

ii) Even if you are unable to identify the exact point of sluggy access you could buy some of the copper tape widely available for slug control and stick a length of it beneath the outside door and also inside the door frame. Then run a strip along the base of the skirting board on outside walls. Refer to *Copper* (above) for more.

(iii) Set your alarm for the middle of the night to catch them out. They come out at night when it is dark, so you will have to do the same until you find them all. Then make a concerted effort to find their access point (vii).

(iv) Set a simplified Beer Trap. Place a deep dish full of beer in the area where slug slime is observed most often, and wait until the morning to find what awaits you.

(v) Leave the lights on.

(vi) Don't leave any food on the floor, or anywhere near the outside walls of a house. Slugs have an incredible sense of smell.

(vii) Possible access points, apart from obvious gaps in the wall or door frame, include:

- Through airbricks.
- Gaps around the pipes in a timber floor.
- Gaps around outlet pipes.
- The fireplace.
- Sink plugholes. Leave the plug in, and weigh it down if necessary, because slugs are extremely muscular for their size.
- Sink overflows.
- Washing machine and tumble dryer vents.
- Use sealant to fill any gaps you can find in the external wall. Look very carefully, inside and out, because a slug can get through a gap of just a few millimetres. Check inside your kitchen unit cupboards too.

Snakes

Many snakes like to eat slugs, although if you have a garden pond they will also seek out young and small frogs. Garden, or garter snakes are among the best ones to encourage, being harmless to humans but very effective slug predators. They will tend to be encouraged by a similar environment to amphibians, and go to hide in any rocky areas, especially around garden ponds for example. Snakes normally avoid humans, so you simply need to get in the habit of running a long stick around any area of the garden which you plan to visit, just before weeding or cutting the grass.

Soapy Water

As a method of killing slugs, you can use soapy water to drown slugs quickly, the soapiness preventing them from climbing the sides. Add a lid, preferably of the screw cap variety, if you want to make absolutely sure. If you put them in a bucket of regular tap water they will do the obvious thing and climb right out. When using soapy water, consider what you plan to do with it next. Pouring into the compost heap is fine, but use eco-friendly soap liquid.

Soldier Beetles

Also known as leatherwings, the larvae of soldier beetles seek out slug eggs and young slugs to eat, while as adults they will continue to be beneficial to your garden with their diet of aphids, You can attract soldier beetles by growing goldenrods, as well as marigolds, large daisies and plenty of herbs, which are leatherwing magnets while blooming.

Spiders

It is a myth that large spiders will include slugs in their diet, although they may eat above ground slug eggs. There is an element of truth in it, however, because harvestmen, or daddy longlegs, look like spiders superficially and are in fact members of the arachnid family. You may well see harvestmen eating a slug, if you are lucky, and these creatures are to be encouraged.

Spray recipes
Ammonia Spray

Mix one part household ammonia with four parts water, no stronger than that. Although too much ammonia is not advisable on your soil, it is composed mainly of nitrogen and even a frequent use of this ammonia solution sprayed directly on slugs should only be harmful to the slug. You could also put this same solution in a bucket to kill slugs quickly, more likely from the ammonia than from drowning.

Buttermilk Spray

Combine one part buttermilk with four parts flour, adding one pint (0.47 liters) of water for each ounce (28.35g) of flour. Spray or use a watering can to coat slugs with this deadly mixture which will encrust them. If you are squeamish and not of a sadistic nature then this is greatly preferable to using salt, as well as being less damaging to the soil.

Caffeine Spray
You can make caffeine spray, using any commercially available spray bottle, cleaned thoroughly then refilled with a very, very strong pot of coffee. As reported in Nature magazine, June 2002, you will need twenty to thirty times the strength of a regular brew (normally .05 - .07%)*, so that the percentage of caffeine is at least 1%, or even 2%. Spray this around your garden at dusk and await the results in the morning. As slugs and snails do not necessarily feed every day, contrary to popular opinion, it is advisable to proceed with this method weekly rather than daily, and you should see a steady decline in your garden's slug population within a few weeks.

However, with the increased strength of this caffeine solution compared with everyday coffee grounds, you should be careful not to spray directly onto or very close to some prized plants as it could hinder plant growth.

"At high concentrations this stimulant becomes a lethal neurotoxin to garden pests....We have discovered that solutions of caffeine are effective in killing or repelling slugs and snails when applied to foliage or the growing medium of plants. Because caffeine is a natural product and is classified by the US Food and Drug Administration as a GRAS ('generally recognized as safe') compound3, it has potential as an environmentally acceptable alternative toxicant for the control of slugs and snails on food crops." (quoted from *Pest Control: Caffeine as a repellent for slugs and snails, Nature magazine, 27 June 2002*).

Garlic Spray
(see _Garlic_)

Horseradish Spray
Boil 3 pints (1.42 liters) of water to the boil, then add half a cup (0.12 liters) of cayenne pepper, 1/2 an inch (1.27cm) of chopped horseradish root, along with 1 cup (0.24 liters) of scented geranium leaves. Allow this mixture to brew for an hour, then strain it and employ your deadly spray.

Isospropyl Spray
(see _Isopropyl Alcohol_)

Quack Grass Spray
(see _Quack Grass_)

Quassia Spray
(see _Quassia Tree Shavings_)

Vinegar Spray
(see _Vinegar_)

Ssukcha
A traditional Korean drink that also has uses as a natural herbicide.
(see _Wormwood tea_)

Starlings
Depending on where you live, you can create an inviting environment for the slug-eating starling to over-winter in your locale by providing nest boxes and planting such shrubs and trees as berberis, crab apple, cotoneaster, holly, and rowan. Starlings will also eat leatherjackets and other pests.

The Sugar Solution
A similar concept to the Beer Trap, you can create a sugary temptation by combining a teaspoon each of lemon juice, jam, and sugar in a glass of water, stirring all the while until the mixture has dissolved. Research has shown the effectiveness of a sugary solution as a highly enticing slug attractant. Now pierce a coke can or similar in the side towards the top, so that the liquid won't spill out, and open the holes into slits which a slug can access, pushing any sharp edges inside the can. The sweet smell should attract slugs, but once inside they then meet their doom from the acidic lemon juice. You can adjust the proportion of lemon juice if any slugs are surviving your concoction, but be careful not to swamp the sweet aroma.

Sweet Gum Tree (*Liquidambar*)
Many people consider the hard, spiky seedpods which drop in their hundreds from Sweet Gum trees in the fall as a serious nuisance. It's true, but they are an even more serious nuisance for slugs. If you know where you can collect a good quantity of these spiny fruits, perhaps wearing thick gloves, then you will have an excellent slug barrier to arrange around your prized plants.

Sweet Woodruff
This is a known slug deterrent which, if grown around your most attractive plants, should reduce slug attacks.

Swiss Chard
The red-leaved Swiss chard variety is an excellent example of a natural barrier that you could use in large quantities to protect your more precious plantings. Slugs are not fond of red-leaved plants and will tend to avoid them and go elsewhere.

Talcum Powder
This can be used in quantity to form a dry surface which slugs have difficulty in traversing (see dry surfaces).

Thrushes
Mainly insectivorous, but thrushes will also eat slugs, though more partial to snails and earthworms. To attract thrushes and similar birds to your garden you can try regularly scattering your garden with small bread crumbs, raisins, and perhaps some wild bird food which you can buy online or at garden centers.

As long as you have hedges and plenty of trees in the vicinity, especially those producing berries for their winter diet, then thrushes and other birds should be happy to stay around and help you control your slug population.

Toads

To attract amphibians such as frogs, toads and newts if you don't have a pond, you need do nothing more than provide a pile of assorted rocks and logs in a shady area of the garden, preferably close to an area of undergrowth. Also try to engineer a small area where rainfall can collect. You may be surprised how quickly they will make this their home, to emerge at night for a tasty morsel of slug. You will probably not even notice them unless you are in the habit of taking an evening stroll in the garden, but you should see a reduction in your slug population.

A great example of nature in harmony - slugs like eating tasty things in your garden, and so do amphibians. It just so happens that their idea of a tasty thing is a slug, and you are merely placing them closer to their food source. Give yourself a pat on the back!

Be warned, however, if you have cats. They like eating - or 'playing with' - amphibians just as much as with any other small creature, so you may find an unwelcome increase in body parts of dead animals in your home. Unfortunately, it seems that slugs are not on a cat's menu.

Traps

If you have a suitable bait (chicken mash would be a good start because of its effectiveness and also for wildlife safety) then it is important that you set the trap correctly. If you are using a covered trap such as a piece of cardboard about 10 inches (25.4cm) square, or perhaps an upturned plant pot saucer, then you must place this above your bait as the evening dampness creeps in. Just as the slugs are coming out to feed. Then be sure to inspect your trap early in the morning, particularly if the day is dawning bright and warm. This will encourage the slugs to leave the warm environment and seek some cool shade. You definitely don't want you slug population to gorge on your bait and then leave before you manage to get your (gloved) hands on them.

Alternatives to this form of safe, non-lethal, baited trap are the _Beer Trap_ - or just _Yeast_ and Water - the _Comfrey_ Trap, other types of Trap, using the _Know Where They Are_ method. Consider using any of these traps sometimes in combination with each other: _Bark Chippings_ - _Beer Batter_ - _Bin liner_ - _Cabbage_ - _Cat Food_ - _Chicken Mash_ - _Citrus Fruit_ - _Coconut Shells_ - _Compost_ - _Cornmeal_ - _Crop varieties_ - _Dog Food_ - _Grape Juice_ - _Melon_ - _Milk_ - _Petroleum Jelly_ - _Slate_ - _Sugar Solution_. More information on each of these can be found in the appropriate place in this book.

Turtles

Some breeds of turtle are slug predators. If there is a turtle habitat close by to where you live then you could have an easy method of slug disposal the natural way. As long as you are prepared to transport live slugs to where the demand is!

Vaseline
see *Grease*

Vermiculite
Try sprinkling vermiculite on the soil around your plants. Slugs dislike moving across it, and if you also dig it into the soil vermiculite will act as a soil conditioner. A win-win.

Vinegar
A non-invasive method of eradicating slugs, best approached by mixing distilled white vinegar in equal parts with water and spraying the solution directly on slugs as you find them.

The best time to go on a slug hunt with spray bottle in hand is after dark. Be careful not to spray plants at the same time, however, as the vinegar will act as a herbicide. Incidentally, vinegar, or a vinegar solution, will also remove unsightly slug slime from your paving.

An additional use for your vinegar is to use it regularly to clean any copper barriers you have set up in your slug prevention efforts.

Water

A little bit contrary this one, as we know that slugs are attracted to damp conditions. Bear with me on this, because this counter-intuitive method can work in regions which are not relentlessly damp and where you can anticipate some warm sunshine. So you should make a point of watering your garden in the morning.

First of all, you may spot some slugs quite soon and be able to pick them off at will - or you could leave that job to nearby bird life. But the main point is that the watered garden will dry out quite dramatically throughout the day under reasonable sunshine, which will leave the slugs desperate for somewhere shady and damp to head towards. They need damp areas in which to survive - and to lay their eggs - so you can hunt them down in those areas, or find, after a period of repeated morning watering that they choose to go elsewhere. Your neighbors won't necessarily thank you for it.

WD-40

The miraculous WD-40 has yet another use, as a slug barrier. Spray it around the sides of your plant containers in the garden from the bottom to at least halfway up. Take great care when spraying, partly to ensure that there are no gaps for slugs to exploit, and also to make sure that you protect your plants from the spray. You should find that this will prevent slugs from climbing up, and as WD-40 is waterproof it will remain in place even after rain, and last for the whole season of major slug activity.

Wormwood Tea

Also known as *Mugwort Tea*, or by its original Korean name of *Ssukcha*, wormwood tea (made from artemisia leaves) has a plentiful supply of Vitamin A and Vitamin C, as well as other health-giving minerals. It has been credited with relief for the common cold, as well as reducing fevers and inflammation, and even with lowering blood pressure.

It interests us here, however, because it can also be used to repel slugs, being a natural herbicide. In fact if you dig it into your soil in slug-infested regions during the fall it will be likely to kill them and their eggs over the winter months.

You can make your own wormwood tea by gathering some wormwood, mugwort, sagebrush or a local type of artemisia for one brimful cup - or bucket, depending on the size of your problem.

Now you should steep this for 24 hours or more in warm water with a ratio of one part wormwood to four parts warm water. Strain the liquid, then add some liquid castile soap containing potassium hydroxide. Make this to a ratio of one-sixteenth castile soap to one part wormwood (a tablespoon for each cupful).

Next dilute the entire mixture to a ratio of one part to another four parts water. Now you have your potent slug deterrent spray for the soil and to directly repel slugs.

Yeast

As referred to earlier, we know that slugs are attracted to the yeast in beer, but if you don't want to waste good beer or are teetotal, then an alternative is a beer-like recipe. Simply put, a well-stirred mixture of baking yeast, sugar and warm water, will ferment and give off a powerful yeasty smell which slugs will find intensely attractive. Perhaps not as attractive as beer, lacking its barley smell, but it should still be a successful slug trap.

Referring back to the experiment for slug beer preferences described under the *Beer Trap* section, the results showed a 50% preference for a yeast mixture compared with the favored beer. However, Coors was shown to be pretty much on a par with a yeasty mixture in this particular test. So for extra slug appeal you could also try adding a little milk to the yeast mixture, and experiment with using honey instead of sugar. In either case, the mixture should turn nice and foamy when it ferments. If you see no foam or any sign of bubbles forming after 30 minutes or so then you will need to warm it all up, stopping well short of boiling or you will kill the yeast.

AFTERWORD

So now you have the tools at your disposal you should experiment with a range of options, test your results, adapt and make progress in your plan to rid your garden of as many slugs as you need to. Remember, though, that slugs and snails have as much right to life as any other creature, and they really can be quite cute.

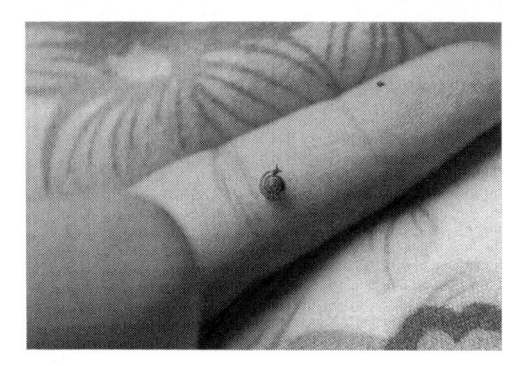

BIBLIOGRAPHY

Wildlife Gardening
by Martyn Cox
ISBN 9780756650896

The Gardeners' Book: For the Gardener Who's Best at Everything
by Diana Craig
ISBN 9781843173274

Pests of the West: Prevention and Control for Today's Garden and Small Farm
by Whitney Cranshaw
ISBN 9781555914011

200 No-work Garden Ideas
by Joanna Smith
ISBN 9780600618652

Pest Control: Caffeine as a repellent for slugs and snails
Robert G. Hollingsworth, John W. Armstrong & Earl Campbell, Nature magazine, 27 June 2002

PICTURE CREDITS

Abax Parallelepipedus Beetle picture {{PD-1923}} by Edmund Reitter (1845-1920), courtesy of Wikimedia
Violet Ground Beetle picture, courtesy of www.wpclipart.com

You can read more about slug control including up-to-date information and new products at our website
www.slugprevention.com

Printed in Great Britain
by Amazon